BERRIES FOR SINGING BIRDS

Eileen Casey

BERRIES FOR SINGING BIRDS

ARLEN
HOUSE

Berries for Singing Birds

is published in 2019 by
ARLEN HOUSE
42 Grange Abbey Road
Baldoyle
Dublin 13
Ireland
Phone: +353 86 8360236
Email: arlenhouse@gmail.com

978–1–85132–217–6, paperback

International distribution by
SYRACUSE UNIVERSITY PRESS
621 Skytop Road, Suite 110
Syracuse
New York
USA 13244–5290
Phone: 315–443–5534
Fax: 315–443–5545
Email: supress@syr.edu
www.syracuseuniversitypress.syr.edu

Typesetting by Arlen House

Cover artwork:
'The Gift' by Sarah Siltala
is reproduced courtesy of the artist
www.sarahsiltala.com

CONTENTS

BERRIES FOR SINGING BIRDS

ASTRONOMER ON THE 15TH FLOOR
Hilton, Lexington

To the left, the Hyatt building with fiery eyebrow
above grounded stars, tail-light constellations.
Cars and trucks map concrete paths.

Blue light switches on below my heart, shadows
my lover's face across galaxies, cloud and sea.
Already half a day ahead, lunch sandwiches eaten.

Winter grimes his skin as he climbs telegraph poles
or burrows beneath pale earth, mending wires.
Weather broken communication.

Streetlamps are globes, burgeoning
a pawnshop's three moons, morning
in hock to a January sky.

Breath from the mouths of pedestrians
steams towards Starbucks where I too
will soon be sipping coffee, straining
to hear what it is people talk about
in a strange city at 8am.

Yesterday a woman asked me my whereabouts,
where I got my coat, 'so pretty, honey'
(like my Irish accent).

Two men in business suits named a foal
whose hooves someday will beat like pulsars
on a paddock out in Keeneland where grasses mauve
towards spring, dog roses not yet bloomed,
tracked by cardinals red as Mars.

CALLISTEMON
for Rebecca

Choked by other shrubs, its brief season
spills over a neighbour's fence – who has the best of it –
seeks out space, sipping days of red.

The last time I saw you, daughter, there was a bronco
stallion of a moon, bucking neon skies
above Times Square. Young men asleep in doorways,
faces beautiful as any Michelangelo sculpture.

I scarcely bore city noises, thrums of wasps.
The apartment in Brooklyn, hot as an oven,
your cat watching birds swoop by windows.
He's seldom been outside; yesterday in his carrier
he pissed with fright on the subway to the vet,
Brooklyn to Coney Island
– you told me in a text. I could almost hear it hiss
across time and light from you to here.

With taut washing line I could strain back
my straying mare, a lasso made where worries,
regrets roam free – but its tendrils are shaped

the very same as wiry filaments that washed
your baby bottles; my fingernail skimming
rims for soured milk. Last Friday's blue moon,
named for two full moons in the same month,
curved a memory of my nursing breast, soft
sucks of your breathing as I kept your airwaves free.

DAMAGE (I)

Woken by sounds of blown-out glass,
busted car horn bleating. Under yellow streetlight
we were a confusion of limbs, pale hands fisted.
Furry slippers, dressing gowns pulled tight.

Firemen came, unwound news-reels.
Miles of it hissed over scorched metal.

As we slept the moon split open – spilled
millions of icy crystals over rooftops;
glanced off smoke-misted bricks,
blackened daffodils,
heavy enough to stick.

When things quietened down we went back to bed.

This unexpected fall sprouted stubble
of a sandpapery texture on a burnt-out car

as if the engine ticked over
under its flipped-up bonnet

might at any moment roar to life,
skid across fresh-laid track.

DAMAGE (II)

As we slept the moon split open – spilling.

Woken by sounds of blown-out glass,
we were a confusion of limbs, pale hands fisted.
Firemen came, un-wound news-reels.

Millions of icy crystals over rooftops,
on the sandpapery texture of a burnt-out car,
blackened daffodils,

miles of it hissed over scorched metal,
heavy enough to stick.
Skid across fresh-laid track.

This unexpected fall sprouted stubble
under its flipped up bonnet;

any moment might roar to life,
glance off smoke-misted bricks.

When things quietened down we went back to bed,
furry slippers, dressing gowns pulled tight,
as if still the engine ticked over, busted
car horn bleating under yellow streetlight.

FIRST CUT
for Alex

Your hair tells the world royal lineage.
Were you an ancient Gaul?
Darker shades for chieftains of the tribe.

Child,
you possess the hue of King Conchobar
in the Tain Bó Cúailnge. Not yet three
years old, shoulder-length waves
grant warrior strength.

Playschool beckons. A hairdresser in a salon
sculpts your baby curls.
New mown grass reins in wayward nature,
scents the air with summer promise.
It must be done.
The same is true of a child's first hair-cut.

Afterwards,
all grown up, you seem taller, thinner.
You stare in the wall-to-wall mirror
at this puzzle of a shorn head.

I gather downy curls, a golden fleece
snagged on the wire of a salon floor.

Years ago, we cut our children's hair ourselves
– a rite of passage ancients called *barbatori*,
binding cutter to the cut.

I wait for re-growth.

My little king.
My little warrior.
My little warrior king.

DRAGON AT THE BOTTOM OF MY TEA CUP

Tufted leaves from Prague, shape-shifted
city of baroque skylines. Dragon, you might

awaken any moment, claw a way out.

I photograph you in my still-warm cup,
faithful to the narrative of happy-ever-afters
in this tealeaf maze. Too well I know
how patterns, like vows, dissolve.

Three days pass. Stubborn, you cling
to the porcelain, bewildered beast
washed-up in an Irish suburban kitchen.

What prophesies can you tell me?
Bright flames already quench in powdery
dregs of this familiar web.

Once proud. Magical. You deserve
so much more than curled around the cold
narrow bed of this cup.

No use searching for a change in fortune.
Now the princess and her children
no longer live in the palace, the prince
written out of their fairytale.

FISHING WITH MY FATHER

We set off through the woods,
dusk breathing through the trees.
We know shape and scent. Oak
whispers to oak, ash to ash, guiding
our path towards the lake.
A slow wind rises. Father sings.

His voice is purply coloured, deep and clotted
like blackcurrant jam, and his song fills
all the empty spaces of this late summer's evening.
I hum along with him.

At the shore I flick my wrist, cast my line
out into rippling waters – as I've been taught
through father's mime. But now it's for real.
A real rod. Real water. Real fish.

Fireflies bat around our heads, midges
stir near the surface, coax brown trout
to fattening feast.
I listen for sudden splashes, but father's
first to feel the tell-tale tug, his body rigid
as he reels in his wriggling catch.

Steel hooks glint through the gashed mouth,
rocks on the shore become a makeshift altar.
Father bludgeons his silver prize
until its writhing, at last, ceases.

Coming back through the woods
fish slimes my hands, fills my nostrils.
Darkness spreads like a stain, drops its
black caul over the lake, across jagged
stones. Our torches barely a match for it.

My father again takes up his song
from where he left it in the trees.
I remain silent as we pass through,

under the cold eye of the moon.

INNISKEEN VISIT

Us, rosy from weather.
The wren hunted and buried.*
Everything said that could be said;

that man from the town who wrung
our turkey's bobbling neck,
shades of a neighbour we once knew
who threw down his letters from England unread,
no money folded in the envelope.

Stirring such embers brings our own father
who delivered those long-ago letters.
Kavanagh, too, flares briefly

reading newspapers on the steps of Jones' Butchers
ruffling the pages into the gutter.

Everything that could be said was said
– Inniskeen's susceptibility to cyclones,
an earthquake alert every fifty years or so;
enough time since the poet's passing
to set us counting.

On a day when the year turns a fresh sod
we plant our feet into damp December soil,
each of us huddling into our own small commotions.
We long for quakes perhaps, or wanting back
familiar rituals that shake the clay off the hours.

* The wren is blamed for betraying the Christian martyr St Stephen,
so hunting the wren takes place on St Stephen's Day.

ACHILL IN OCTOBER
for Ellen

At curdled sea's edge sandpipers
rush to shore. Pale feathers
wave and wade in water's
reflection. Conjoined
lollipop stick legs.

Skies mingle
mist, sea-spray.
Smoke
wisps upwards
mirror imaged
mountains.

Beachcombers
print trails
washed clean
by incoming
tide.

In the hills
cottages steal
shade from clouds,
a curlew pokes the reeds.

Your birthday daughter
dated on the sands
marked out by driftwood
circled by a heart.
Smudged as lipstick
after a night out.

Photographed upside down;
reminder how you breeched the world.
Diving in, feet first.

MAN MELTING
at the Red Line Luas terminus, Tallaght

It's cold enough to snow. Wind whips down
Dublin Mountains, skins spaces between
buildings. Bare legs purple like heather.

Druggies shuffle the platform, cadge cigarettes,
shake empty cups under the noses of strangers
who turn to other strangers, make small talk.
Rub the genie lamp of conversation. Weather.
Headlines in newspapers.

Even the world of soap has more veracity
than this brave new world. Apartment block
totems against charcoal skyline.

Breath steams out towards empty shells nearby,
ghost buildings once rocketed into boom and bust.
Windows are spidery; webbed with glass
splintered in the night by flying bricks.

From granite-limbed arches comes a scarecrow,
a man in a stained black tracksuit, hair grime
slimed, marbles for eyes.

The Luas opens its doors to the promise of warmth.
The driver's voice booms out:
*'Will the man dressed in black and carrying a sack
please desist from boarding. You have been travelling
up and down the track all morning, sir'.*

Without protest, he turns back, head hunkered
like a tortoise into hunched shoulders.

We board the Luas. Carriages fill up. Settle
into eye-line zones. We skim clean hedgerows,

housing estates slide by, each passing mile
takes us further away from a man's broken shoes
flapped against filthy under soles; a man melting.

ORANGES

April winds and the lure of fruit
drive me home. Of all temptations –
crisp loaves, fuzzy peaches – oranges
bulge from my shopping bag.

I unpeel gloves, coat, scarf,
drop them carelessly on the hallstand
like underwear on a bedroom floor.

The mirror shows me a cold-eyed woman
split into two segments, one half
in the glass, museum piece preserved,
other half sinew and bone.

In my north-facing kitchen, I nestle the oranges
into a porcelain bowl, careful as if a clutch
of new-laid eggs. Breast soft, goose pimpled
rind swaddles over what lies at its centre
once I pierce its outer layer.

I lift one out, prick its skin until juice

drenches my fingers, drifts
bitter sweet scent towards my lips.

PAPER

Stripped from wood, mulched clear water soft
faced southwards, elements exposed to dry.
Stability of sunlight determines shadow crop;
water, light, eye, blue sky retreating shy.
Too much, too thin. Too little, too thick.
No wonder birds flock or oceans purl.
Smoky shavings torch horizons wick
charcoal reminders of shaving curls.
Pounded, immersed, impurities cleansed,
a girl writes her story on swallow pages
strung with peacock fibre's feathery blend
while behind a Mino screen, her sages
silhouette her shape, veined watermark
writes melancholy memory of bark.

SNOWDROP

We strain for first spring sight of you,
as we do in the airport each time
our daughter strides through *Arrivals*.

Such long months of absence, scarcely
a letter. Green duffle bag packed tight,
enough inside to tide her over – two weeks
at most. Her short season ends in *Departures*.

Snowdrop, you give us reason to hope.
A shy flower, cossetted in earth,
you pierce frosted ground,
test for weather. Always a startle
to see you appear. Snowdrop,

in the wake of luminous graces,
console us with your elegant traces.

So Long, MaryAnne

A struggle of light on grass softens
early morning frost, stiff blades

cajoled towards melt. A pheasant's
long tail spouts out behind him.
His head twitches the ground,
dawn light pecks at trees.

In the hills, cattle and horses steam
above silent cottages. A cow stampedes.

Has she heard Leonard Cohen's died?

Lyrics sung to her flanks as hands
pump the tune on an organ of teats.
Warm milk squirted into buckets
silvered with song.

Four O'Clock Flower

Unnoticed in daylight,
drab petals fold stem tight.
No clues cue your presence,
forced to bide your time

like a vampire in his lair sulks
towards slow time dusk.

Morning creeps by. Late afternoon
dims noon. You flare to life,

centre stage in your theatre, spot lit
by evening's crenulation, sharp
scarlet bites. Songbirds parachute
down, marvel at your blood
-thickened tones. *Mirabilis jalapa,*

named for wonder when Aztecs ruled.
Plain in pale sight. Miraculous
revelation, shadow lipped.

True night flower
midnight sipped.

THE POWER OF POEMS

Poems detonate hope in those who are cast down,
who hide in fear along remote hillsides. Poems
are sturdy vessels when put to sea, strong enough
to navigate stormy waves, rebuild war-torn cities
so rubble becomes sturdy foundations. Poems

don't turn a stranger from their door. Won't allow
shame or ignorance to cloud their better judgement.
Poems replenish and revive, offer shelter, food, warmth.
Lend reprieve to those bereft, who fear the sniper
taking aim on rooftops, who smell cordite on the wing.

Poems pour oil on troubled waters, soothe and salve.
Poems dry tears shed in lonely rooms on lonely streets
at daybreak or at close of day. Inspire other poems
in other poets. Poems, with love, conquer fear.
Are healing. Are heard above the roar of gunfire,
battle cries on battlegrounds where guns are loaded.
Greed, lust, hate. Poems go about their business,
light beacons that never will be quenched.
Poems very presences weaken the same unease

fear thrives upon, stirred up by those who never
can be easy. Those who break the homes
and hearts of others. Poems release them
from this cycle. And their children.
And their children's children.

Poems bathe in sunlight yet know the icy chill.
Poems forge a shield for grief
yet make a space for laughter.
Poems, like berries on a rowan tree,
are succulent, rosy food for singing birds,
carrying nurturing seeds of love.

On Bray Beach

A miracle of weather bakes stone loaves.
Trickles ice-cream over fingers and chins.
Bray promenade paints panoramic vistas,
striped awnings, hazy plastics.

Sky-tinged ocean dimples surface folds.
A tease of ebb and flow flirts with pilgrim's
crawl towards Bray Head.

A child goes missing.

Aftershock distorts the frame. Carousels
cease, swing boats bob in empty air.
Sea breezes cease playful rhythms,
windmills motionless.

Bare feet scurry over flesh-prickling shale.

Sentinels string out along the shoreline
caught up in this sudden drama of hide and seek,
search and prowl between gaps in booths
hung with buckets and spades.

Dressed for winter a man sits, his back pressed
against the sea wall staring out, oblivious to how
suspicion already winds the black ribbon, worn
like a funeral band around his Panama hat,

out beyond hotels, seafront houses, into
narrow laneways leading to the town
– shadows dart like minnows.
Suspicion spreads contagion into alleys,
garden sheds, disused outhouses.

Just as quickly as it begins, it ends –
restores reason's syncopated rhyme.
A cry goes up, the wanderer's found.
Relief swells from the sea.

A fresh white wave rolls in.

ONCE UPON A TIME IN TALLAGHT

A woman crosses over a bridge in slow motion.
Cars move under her like a river, in real time.

Dressed in a tweed, double-breasted coat,
she opens her mouth and out comes an aria's
strange pitch. Opera notes sail over
bypass traffic, new hatched birds
no one's heard before. Some nest in trees
near the Dodder, break hearts each spring
when the world is new again yet regrets
stir to life. Fragile as a quail egg.

A woman pushes back time, as if an accordion
played at any speed. Her aria frames sun,
moon and stars. From entrance to exit,
it flows, transforms shopping trolleys into chariots.

This shutter speed colours her world white.
Soft crocuses of snow fall with the notes.

Once upon a time in Tallaght poppies
blooded wild fields, no old bones existed
in this *Tir na nÓg* place. A woman crosses
over a bridge near a supermarket, her aria's
notes, so many, she had not thought so many.

Score for darker days in squall and sprawl.

POUCE
after a photograph taken in 1938 at Lindsay Thompson (Threads Ltd.)
Prospect Mill, Belfast

Two rows of men and women, for all the world
two lines of sentences begun in seeding fields.

Shoulders stooped in clauses between
stook and stack, hackle of steep, stem,
scutch of stinking verbs.

In the lull of this caesura, faces stare into the lens;

a rare breath between comb and card.
In daylight's squaring off
shadowy interiors, scarce glimpsed.

There is a rhythm and a rhyming here
in each sober, sedate pose – *douce* –

recorded by a photographer's monochrome ink.
Older women already appear to fade.
Alveoli, tiny pink balloons, are like seedpods,
swollen to their ordained size.

Brief flowerings drying in the sun.

The photograph is grainy –
as if a layer of dust has settled on the years
and one word – *flax* –
frames it with its true blue
noun.

RESULTS

You are given the all-clear
as if you've circled the skies
seeking permission to land.

Some say you are 'out of the woods';
they sent you weeks ago to a shelter
made from winter leaves. Damp earth.
Where two roads converged.

I went in search of the blue bird of happiness
– its sweet voice, blue moon song.

I lured him with mulberries,
magenta shades of joy,
so he'd spread his blue wings,
let me touch the beat of his blue heart.

But he flew to other skies. Instead
I found faint traces, dead ends.

Until today,
when you tell me what the doctor said.

WISTERIA
Birr Castle Gardens

Snake of wisdom, dove of peace.
Sinewy vines coil naked July pergola
loop warm bread scents plaited into
fresh washed Saturday night hair.

Journeys shiffle these timbers,
bony beginnings and ending,
porthole of branches.

White blends into lavender
pods are poisonous. Wisteria.
Rhymes the woman's complaint,
crab apple breasts, spite glazed.

Outside these Saturday gardens, people
buy Sunday joints, collect dry cleaning.
Snooze in cars on Main Street.

Layers of root drill down into riverbed,
dragon flies dance on lily-pads.

Sunshine hollows out light where lotus
flowers float serene. A fisherwoman flings
out her line. Stirs star spindles in calm waters.
Trees kick up their heels, bury their heads
surrounded by starling swarms.

SUBJUNCTIVE

There is no warning, no funeral in my brain.
Morning's mirror unveils my left eye, drenched
crimson, more exotic bloom than floating lily.
When I look right or left, it prances
across my optic wilderness,
more Bowie than O'Donnell.

The doctor calls such sudden detonation
a Subjunctive Haemorrhage
(Sub H in layman's language), citing
such violent explosion as:
increase in blood pressure, constipation, coughing
sneezing, lifting heavy objects, advancing age.

This sudden *apparition* – his word –
(I do not claim it has the face of Jesus
or any of the saints)
could just as well result from:
laughter (*the belly wobbling kind*)
sex (*strenuous*)
dance (*hip hop, salsa, tango*)
yet, these remain unlisted.
He suggests I wear an eye patch.

No doubt I could. Become
an older New Romantic (my words)
like Boy George or Adam Ant.

Yet, as it fades, lighter shades drop
paler berries into this subjunctive stream;

more silver apples of the moon
than golden apples of the sun.

TALES OF A PARROT

Storyteller, come to us as the crow flies.
Bring news of enchanted lands, Persian
pearled words. We believe in your fables.

Don't bring us fledglings, plump as new suns,
nest fallen. Parents, like hummingbirds
fled to the next source of nectar.

Weave us instead long grasses, banish
predators, betrayal on pecking mouths.

Ease ragged hurts, grant us nomadic
wing spans in an after-sunrise place,
bilberries tempting bell-shaped sounds.

Draw back veils on a wedding morning

as if clearing a mist. Show us the sketch,
a future well planned. Distract us to a skyscraper

forest landscape filled with sunrise.

Even for the span of one day. Filter
scarlet and blue, feathers true.

THE GOOD ROOM

Sofa, lamp, coffee table, cabinet. A construct
in a furniture shop window brings eight of us
squashed inside our two-up-two-down,
three-children-in-a-bed council house. Just so
we could have a parlour. When bad,

we got sent to The Good Room. Rags on knees
to shine, dust and wax our penance. Chirrups
drifted down the sooty tunnel to grate.
Fires, due to blocked chimneys were never lit.

Above the grate embroidered calligraphy hung.
Learn of Me For I Am Meek and Humble of Heart.

A single armchair rooted on either side of the grate,
lace antimacassars covering backs and arms.
The Good Room seemed to belong to a world
bequeathed by grandparents perhaps but we'd
only ever met our father's side. Mother, brought
to the midlands from the west, gaps and silences,
rise and fall of the sea in her voice.

Father from the town seldom asked his brothers
round, and when they came they sat
awkward in the kitchen, sipping lukewarm tea.

The Good Room. Only ten foot by twelve foot.
Ghosted in a shop window. Chirruping
whirlpool echoed down the aboriginal tunnel.

To the Wolf's Door

*Follow the example of the wolf. Even when he is surprised and runs for
his life, he will pause to take one more look at you before he enters his
final retreat. So you must take a second look at everything you see*
                                                    – Dr Charles A. Eastman

Getting here has taken me long as I remember –
back as far as when I stretched on tip toe –
strained even then to lift this iron ring;
woollen shawl and bonnet scratching at my skin.

I feel the burden of this basket, wicker
– same as grandma's chair is made of,
the one she rocks herself to sleep in.

Loaded with pies, baked in noon-day heat.
Mother's apron flapped, cooled them off
fast as she was able, promises and warnings
sealed under glazed crusts;

how I must get a head start,
out-run the wolf, reach that clearing
before a jawbone moon gobbles up
what's left of daylight.

Nor wander off.
Else feel grandma's dying breath
on wolf's smooth talking, lying tongue.

All that juice seeped through all the same,
drew the woodcutter who I've already
shaken off, who would have my curls
on his block if he could, too much gold
for his liking I could tell.

I hear the crackle of twigs disturbed,
taste wolf in water that I drink –

something else I can't be sure of.
I too can read the signs, the small print.
I'll take my chances.

White Fences Make Good Neighbours

I'm painting the fences white, shed too,
white as a gumdrop or a wedding shoe.

When that's done I'll float in a summer palace
canopied by pale-leaved white-beam trees,
lie on a blanket with my ice-coloured cat,
eat cake, be cooled by spigots of light.

I'll read about Antarctica while butterflies
ripen like berries, ignore warning telegrams
pipped by a blackbird,
three tiers up at least.

I'll be whitening out lawnmowers, chainsaws,
barking feuds, a neighbourhood's graffiti of sound.

NIGHT VISIT
for Sarah Siltala

Cluster of grapes
moon glossed blue.
Night bird perches
on porcelain ledge.

In his mouth hangs a blue pearl
juice blown like glass.
Droplet held by stem vein.

Time fans over wings
catches its breath. Such wisdom
mirrors through a vacuous eye.

SHAVE

Seagull dive and splash breaks ice
dimples man-made lake. Memory wing
stirs a morning ritual;

shirt open to the waist, skin a pale watermark
below father's weathered neck.

He'd dip his brush in soap, lather foam
in the red basin. Blades blunt on raw skin,
sharp steel nicked flesh, cuts newspaper dotted.

Wilkinson's Sword, sold in ones and twos,
how he also bought his *Players Please*.

He dipped the brush, shook droplets,
bristles taking aim at his assistant,
rough towel at the ready.

Left and right he'd shift his mouth so the blade
ploughed snowy foam. Pummelled dry,
he slapped two hands across his cheeks,
stoked up rosy fires.

I'd throw the water down the shore,
tide-marks wiped clean.

The seagull rises high into November skies,
swans with cygnets glide by. No room
for sentiment. Soon, full grown, pushed out
they'll find their own universe.

Lake waters settle back to its flat surface.

BLACK SUN, WHITE TREES

Four October birds fly into my suburban garden
arcs of a looped future, sure as the one pale egg
soon to come. Constellations of wing and feather
shield spring sun before it sets
in the marshlands of Denmark.

Without Saint Christopher's blessing they'll surge.
Feathery dolphins swimming skies, blue and green
weaves a shimmer of speckled headscarves,
mesh of women, children on their coat-tails
in a Friday marketplace, swirl in and around
sure as skiers criss-crossing forest tracks
twig thin or fat as an otter's belly
on winter slopes.

In the chemist shop, mothers buy sulphur
to mix with starling droppings,
cure for ringworm, shiny as medals.

AT THE YEATS SUMMER SCHOOL

Is it a curse or a blessing to be an early riser?

Pinked bricks froth on the Garavogue,
dawn-lit barges for fishermen, pints
downed in snugs the night before.

Only 7am. Yeats up with the lark,
quotes and plaques on restaurant gables.
Poets and scholars sailing in dreams,
nowhere visible in this all-too-real world.

Already I've been approached by a beggar.
Passed pleasantries with a road sweeper,
dodged a hose trained on hanging baskets.

Up a side street, a pair of high heels out of shape
on a windowsill stand defiant. Straps broken.
Flanked by empty glasses in a regimented row.
Crushed out cigarettes bloat the dregs.

The girl who went home barefoot, Sligo
streets spread under her feet, probably
sleeps it off or is nursing a 'head' full blown.

Or maybe her story's gone on to another town,
a duplicate set of clues left behind in toe-prints
shaped in tattered leather.

MAGI

We slake our thirst, leave forests tinder dry.
Candles of melting spruce, birch,
crackle songbirds from their perch, fires
blaze unchecked. Heart sore we grieve,

plead for rain, try to mend our ways.

Fallow land slumbers. Scorched earth
struggles to rise above its charred history.
Scutch grasses bristle towards a tender
sky, speckled as an egg, eager to hatch
new moons. We honour your watch

on blackened hills, sprinklings
of powdery ash, a soothing talc
on wounded earth. You bind moss
to spindle bark, transform sludge
to silvery streams, spill pools, sacred
light into hollows charcoal sculpted.

Thrush and swallow return,
blackbirds sing again in lonely hearts.

We honour your watch, your sacred vigil.
You bear witness. You keep track.

PEARL
for Aoife

At last, the troublesome tooth's come loose.
A crater hollowed in your gum
wriggles your soft tongue into its centre,
drawn to its jelly interior

as a babe seeks out the fleshy nipple,
or how the sea is pulled by the moon.

Your cousins cease their play,
sensing a change in your feathers,
you a rosy robin of a girl
– a part of your life
drifted from its moorings
is up for grabs.

These hawks jostle for such treasure,
know the going rate
for such a prize

– how a back molar's value
is not so much or as easily recalled
in photographs.

At the kitchen window gazing out at a garden
bereft of leaves, gapped spaces in trees
earth mulched, I hear a blur of squawk,
pecking beaks at the ready.

The circle becomes a scrum,
bodies tumble over each other
limb on limb, bone on bone.

I tap the glass. Arms and legs
come apart, disgruntled faces bob for air

like apples in Halloween's ducking bucket.
My all-seeing eye is now upon them,
terrible as a cyclops.

I open the back door, you step inside,
lips pressed, like curtains drawn
before Act II of this sudden drama.
Holding your secret for as long as a breath
you unlock the five keys of your fist.

There it lies, embedded in your palm,
ruby tinged, battle scared from its
struggle to remain fixed
in the wobbly depths of your gum.

You open your mouth wide
as a fledgling in the nest. I gauge
crater size and shape
as any grandmother worth her salt.

I nearly but don't
press my finger to the wound
as if to staunch a flow
that's not yet there. Instead
I place the milk tooth in an envelope,
name and date it like a specimen
for safe-keeping.

Until midnight's fairy
takes it from beneath
your dreaming pillow
in exchange for silver.
Your adult tooth, strong as willow
shoots already rooted. Soon to gleam
ghost of pearl.

FROM THE ROYAL SCHOOL

It's a week since I saw the boy King Tutankhamun
put on show in Dublin. Taken from his resting place
inside three coffins – in turn housed in four containers
leafed in golden hieroglyphics. Replicas all,

as if the past might be constructed from old photographs
settled under glass. Left in total darkness,
until layers unpeel beyond a golden mask.
Under that again, wrapped in linen shrouds
eyes, ears, nose and mouth.
Here in Armagh, I'm bound to be reminded
by the smallest thing no less, a clump of petals,
withered on the path, fallen out of hanging basket
like a yellow chick from its nest.

Bringing me love notes all the same,
strewn by a child bride before the lid was closed.

In the Royal School, that first night's sleep tears
on briars. Finding peace in a strange place.
I wake to Harold's Cross, hear traffic rumbling by.
Headed towards the city of my eighteenth year.

A narrow, single bed takes me to present tense.
I reach for ghost warmth. My husband's sleeping back.
This small window tells me how little or how much
I piece together that makes sense.

A town is a town is a town is a town. I can pull my blind
up or roll it down.

From these remnants I sew. Curving pathways
flanked by green. A wild bird, mysterious Ibis?
Or just a solitary crow pecking for an early worm
as my pen pecks at blank pages.

That bird is usurped at evening by pigeons –
roosting in McGarry's shed in the midlands
where I come from – forcing out such guttural sounds.

Across tracks of green and time, houses lean together
gossiping in mime. Beyond those houses a rush of angles,
streets shield each other from full view.
Scarce a glimpse of moon.
Muscles in my thighs feel the steep rise to Market Square.
Armagh Cathedral. Bearings taken from the launderette at
its gates boasts 'squeaky clean' while collapsing. Into ruin.

My window sill is wide enough to sit upon. If Lancelot
comes I will gladly gaze upon his trace. For I've not seen
one living soul pass beneath these panes.
Only swallows gorging on the wing for flying south.

The Royal School seals me in. Stairwell swaddles.
Each one leads to another story. Across the mall are names
inscribed in stone, names I knew the childhood taste of:
Smith, Durcan, Talbot, Delaney, Walsh, Daly, Boyce,
Wilson, McNally, McCarthy and O'Neill.

Voices silenced now, this monument a meeting place.
Young men and women stake their claims to life and love,
children play on the canon as if it were an iron horse
riding out at noon or grazing, staying put.

It's that time of year too. End of summer bricking itself up,
dresses in the shops touched by strangers are marked
down, soon-to-be covered in polythene. Put in storage.

I half expect to see my mother in Armagh. These streets
appear the same as home.

A town is a town is a town is a town. Or, a neighbour long
since dead.

Sarah Purcell. Her blue black hair, the one luminous thing
glinted under sunlight. A woman whose sleeves rolled
to the elbow. Who kept her legs, arms and head bare.
Breathing every bit of air.

Her house was the last one on our road to be connected,
electricity flooding into places used to flickering shadows.
Unsettling her for days. Breaking up her words
in strangest ways.

HARE
Annaghmakerrig, July 2019

When the shutters fold back
I'm sound-proofed behind glass.
Swans on the lake flutter
white flags, only breath I see.

You look up; berry-eyed,
pert as a young girl's breast.
See me framed. Just out of bed
creases in my skin.

We stare at each other, unsure
of our footing, not wanting
to pierce the thin veil between
your world and mine suffused
by a shock of green love.

Distracted, perhaps by a wren's
chick chick, you turn away.
I follow, like Oisín into the opening
of a tree just beyond a thicket
where a wild bird's song
rests on a lupin's purple hue;

hoping to find the princess, her blood
drizzled into dry earth. Blessed as rain.

Wish Bone

We pull this bone as we did

when we were sister warriors, same
tribe, yet combat locked for luck
skinny as a robin's leg.

Such small victories
saw us through the week,
amulets glazed with pride
snug in a pocket

or tucked inside a school book
drying like a flower.

With the carcass of the bird
picked clean enough
so all trace of meat and gristle
disappeared, we'd grit teeth,

crook our smallest finger
until purchase on the bone,
V-shaped as a diviner's rod

snapped in two
reeled us backwards

as if we'd pulled on an eagle

not a humble boiling fowl
neck wrung two days before.

We never asked what it was exactly
wished for, if granted or refused.

We pull this wishing bone sister,
our fingers thin as a robin's leg,

brittle with passing years,

strength itself thrown off
like liquid from the second boil.

WINTERING GROUND
for John

Lined with newspaper, between layers,
a sauce bottle warm water brimmed,
makeshift incubator. It's the same shoebox
held your father's best pair.

A life ebbs in the cardboard casket,
feathers moonlight pale. A plover!
You know such treasure, how to read

its black-gold markings.

Blackbirds you'd saved before, a robin
so badly mauled you hastened its end.
Holding back tears, how you were taught.

You keep vigil through the night,
as at the hospital short months before;

plover's breath weakening towards dawn.

You charted its journey flown from skies
drenched by *aurora borealis*,
dyeing the sky glorious shades;

bitter winds left behind to reach
milder weather; where rivers flow
unchecked. Daylight bleeds

through gaps in the outhouse roof.
One last exhale. Eyes glazed.

You lift the bird, his still warm body
soft against your frozen cheek.

SEA HAWK

Diving osprey, silk ballet shoes spear the air,
hands splayed for the white fingers of the catcher.

Trapeze artists know everything depends
on these split seconds and, like binary stars,

circle each other above sawdust shavings
smells of elephants, creaking boards

rows of upturned faces.

The last thing you want when out on a limb
is that heron stood in inches of ice
or the water hen pecking at her frozen surface
not making much of a dint,
riding it out until it's over.

You want the sea hawk in ballet shoes
pointed towards you

when you leave that metal strip
ground rushing up.

TRACKS

Arrows in the snow
scarce an indent

trails from wild bush
to sombre tree.

Berries glisten,
swollen red.

Beneath hard earth
worms fatten to surface
lured by dancing claws.
Two crows, dark silhouettes
stark against a blur of white.

Beaks sharpened to burst skin
pink. Feast on juicy entrails.

A tiny robin, brittle thin
as a late December day
rounds the rose on his chest
a lantern barely lit, waits for crumbs.

Deep in the forest, bird of crow tribe,
jay skitters across the forest floor
gathering acorns in his throat pouch.
Hoard bag for treasures stockpiled.

Shy bird, his screaming call flies
between woodland trees. Blue
pink and black plumage flashes
mark him out. He hides his stash
under dry leaves, twigs.
Like wise virgins trim wedding lamps.

Word stores ripen over time,
fat with grace. Or wither
in word-starved seasons.

WILLOW MAN
after a visit by Michael Hartnett to Virginia House, Tallaght

He arrived late in a pre-booked taxi but I would have waited
longer even for that first glimpse of him leaning
through the doorway as if a birthing taking place,
shoulders coming first, then the rest.

This small, dark man with brooding eyes,
tweed jacket, cap peaked as a diviner's rod.

Half-in, half-out, he seemed unsettled
like a foal first finding its awkward stride.
His voice grown strong,

clear well water, child-like magic
spilled from his mouth.

Poems drifted outside where willow branches
wound pathways, as voices he connected up
from the Telephone Exchange in Exchequer Street.
It must have pleased him, conversations
flying on witcheries of wire through air.

That tree, symbol for wisdom, *Salix*
(he knew its Latin name)
is long gone. As is Virginia House.
Replaced by shape-shifting landscape.

A Luas line snakes its way to a city of many tongues.
We are different yet the same since he was here.

Dublin Mountains tower still behind our houses,
thrushes sing with wrens in Gleann na Smól,
winds sweep away winter ghosts,
moon and stars sickle our skies,
willow roots, like language itself, go deep.

MUTE
for Cathal

Little boys shout tom-a-hawk whoops.
Calliopes letting off steam.
Not this. Blank, no speech world.

Little boy. You are a salmon, word-spawn
full. Words that startle wild horses
to gallop. Slide down snowy hills.
Words marbled bright, shiny, stripped,
chequered. Ivy covered, climbing
one to another. Creepy-crawly thick words.

Little boy. Swimming against currents,
silvery tongued yet you scarce make a splash.

In dreams I slit you tail to throat.
Out they spill, your shiny hoard.
Words like:
'Love', 'Grandmother'
fall into my empty net.

THE TREACHERY OF IMAGES
Ceci n'est pas une pipe

I

Fill it with desire, it smells of gunpowder. Or words.
Spewed from its wide mouth onto hard, cold surfaces.
Few survive the impact.

An Emperor Penguin arrives on Peka beach,
mistakes sand for snow. This is not a pipe. Nor this
gondola the same one clambered into day after day.
Cities are crumbling, washing lines slack across years.
A man and woman grow old.

II

End of war; the weather inclement for strawberries.
The woman longs for trickling juice, paints her nails red,

brightens an armchair's dark covers. Old boots, earth
wedged, lean against the hot spice of a winter kitchen.
The man counts globes of cellulite-skinned fruit, smoke
and turf dust swirled in skillets of four and twenty hours
baked in the pies of summers past. Days were shorter then.
They sat together at a sunburnt table,
radio playing. In the yard, the man sliced a stump of wood
in two, snagged his flesh on its pimpled drifts.

III

The shutter speed is set slow to take down time itself a peg
or two, snow tripped branches bright, background blurred.
Here there is silence in the frame and a sleeping child
swaddled against winter. Spring thaw is near.
The man wears a good tweed suit, the woman wishes
blue light to stream across a deck chair, split herself in half.

IV

Five years later, the man is on a beach with his blue-eyed son.
He carries a stone large as a loaf of the woman's bread, soon
eaten, soon forgotten. The child knows not yet
how hard a stone can be.

V

At end of day, which of them will say:
'This is not real life but a performance for the world of
dust to dust'.
Who will be the first to scrawl a name on the urns of time?

High in the mountains, groves of trees are harvested.
Glistening, an olive catch falls into autumn nets.
A man and woman lie down and love, then fell asleep.
The woman shakes the man awake, first to see his eyes,
luminous at the sight of her. There is comfort in Magritte.

Moon Bird

Crow thieved the moon, thinking it
a seer's eye, his future written all over it.
So much wishing for its gold
eased this orb from its socket,
lifted it clean. It tumbled
to earth unbroken, mystery intact.

A crow black bird starved
night-skies of light, except
for drizzles of stars.

No hunter's moon lantern.
Torch for lovers.

He pecks at his globe with razor beak,
tests it for blood. A hint of blue.
An egg nested inside. Bone of his bone.
The mate, like Eve, he's longed for.

A fabulous version of himself.
Or a cuckoo's hatchling
poised to upset the universe.

All night he's pondered.
Warm it under his breast
or give in to the sea's angry pull?
All he wished for wasted,
dashed off the rocks.

He rolls it playful with its round-
ness. Still, it makes no sound,
shows no crack. Its cold eye stare
fills him with dread. Windfall or curse?
He buries it under rustled leaves
beneath a winter bare tree.

IN SLEEP
for Callum

Like a baby finch, you hum
to sleep. Rhythmic waves
carry you onto dreaming shores.

You learn your songs
in spaces between slumbering breaths.
Feather sprouted sounds
fly you deep.

May you always have wings,
little boy aged two.
Hum. Fly deep. So stars
bright as pearls
light your shell path,
so you always find songs
in blissful sleep.

MEMENTO

Scarlet on white inks her rosy mouth
seals waxy lipstick on a napkin
cast careless on my bed
moons ago now.

'Don't wait up Ma' – preserved
 in tissue paper, a keepsake.

As are shoes and curls,
milk teeth.

Her full lips bring me back.

Sun down, moon rise,
her mouth a curve each tick
on the clockface

sands of time and wicked imaginings.

Settled with the slam of a taxi door,
high heels clumped up the stairs,
sleep welcome as a blackbird's song.

These lips on tissue, like ripe red plums,
youth's plump, fleeting shade.

FROM PHUKET
for Ellen

Texts come in at odd hours
like lovers out on the town.
Time-zone difference, 300 whole
minutes between Phuket and Tallaght.

Enough time to boat trip to Phi Phi
or ride the Luas to an early city street.

Your sun rises earlier than ours;
just as the last of evening powders
down like dried-out insects,
already you're headed for dawn
on the edge of a world chorused by finches.

Videos come in too. Angles distorted.
Trumpet flowers, peach skinned.

You've washed elephants in a sanctuary,
skin wizened like old trees.
Rushes of wind whip through sound
could be the top of a mountain in Killarney
– not this tropical paradise.

Everything's so cheap. Little or nothing.
Bottles of this. Cartons of that. Wrap-overs,
Flip flops. Six euro massage.

Ten days in, everything's still cheap.
Only now you miss home. Familiars.
What went before Bangkok.
Weeks of packing in the small bedroom
above our kitchen; your suitcase a chasm
filled with suncream, summer clothes.

It's the girls. So young.
So many. For sale. Cheap.
Bars. Restaurants.
Street corners. It slicks oil
over new sandals, smears
lotion on new clothes.

TROUBLE WITH OLD HOUSES

Moved out, you leave behind a clock,
stuck on ten after eight. A poster of Rocky
Balboa's bloodied face, one eye half closed,
shoulders hunched, his hands in boxing gloves,
two big red balloons.

Postered beside him, Al Pacino in a white suit,
grey Fedora. Not giving a shit.
Cool as the north wing of this 70s house.

Under the bed, I find sweet wrappers, old coins,
a toy horse, Trojan, stuffed with childhood wounds.

I take down the posters, see the paint's original,
a softening shade penned off, brighter
than what's outside the ring,
where we, old sparring partners
still go one last round.

SENTINELS

Ravens know the etiquette of funerals.
Prize Sunday visits.

Relatives sift out weeds, poke at graves,
pluck stray wisps of gravel birthed
grass. Ravens are to cemeteries
as big black umbrellas to rain.

Raucous, they keen with mourners,
cousins to jays, magpies, birds,
thick beaked enough to spear sparrow

or starling. Cedars cut down, ravens
emigrated to the town, flocked
over rooftops in housing estates.

Among the living, they are less vocal, scarce
worth the bother. No headstones. Swift prayers,
hurried signs of the cross. Steel sliced
cakes of earth, feasts of fat worms.

JORIE GRAHAM'S BRACELETS

They catch the eye and then the ear, a bojangle branganjle
shape and sound swished each time her wrists
turn round, like the volta in a sonnet.
Scarce room to summon
                    Baba Marta's new born spring
                            or Azabache's spell.

Such slidings
      in and out of place
            play hoop-la,
                  stacking and restacking
                        style and grace.

Or like Sisyphus
      roll bone on bone;
            leather, metal, shell
                  up and down
                        the white slopes of her arms.

Octagonal, trapezium, kite, rectangular
these bracelets are collars too. Snares.
Trapping metaphor and image. Portholes to quakes
wake and shake the universe.

Behind a podium, with the microphone turned on
nothing coming back across the footlights
but a blare of silence; these bracelets tell Ms Graham
she is not alone.

Let's hear it for Jorie Graham's bracelets,
the chutzpah with which she wears them
all at once – even if – sometimes they snag her silks
or tangle up her gorgeous hair.

Like rooftops they are studded in moonlight
    slanting sleek across the maps of memory.
        Purchased in exotic sites they sparkle,
          leave a band between the layers

wide enough so poems can sink into white spaces.

At day's end, cooling from her heat,
they jostle together on her bureau while on her bare arms
traces of them breathe, luminous in the dark.

DIG

A man and a woman are found,
holding tight to each other

as if it were yesterday they died
– not 5,000 years ago.

Two Neolithic celebs exposed
to a world keeping up with Kardashians;

a world where it's no longer two by two,
one of each, into the global ark.
Who knows what the pick prises open?

Mistress and lover?

A blade still glints in this burial chamber
as if newly plunged into flesh.

The scene reeks with memory of bodies

stripped back to bone. Forbidden
fruit tasted in Eden grown from seed
nourished by illicit deed.

Two bodies, in truth, now too dead
to feel lust, suspicion or blame,
denial or shame. Crumbled to dust.

Husband and wife? Guilty as charged.
Their crime? Putting each other through

a lifetime of love.

LITTLE PIRATE
for Saoirse

Your good eye in hiding behind plastic shield.
Lazy one exposed slides towards the centre,

a lopsided version of an argument

veered off-course. Intent
on getting its own way,
it passes down the genes.

Some call it 'turned' or 'crossed'.
Worse names for shields, cotton

patches, glassless spectacles.
Optical eclipses in bedside locker,
hoarded reminders of a childhood
half the frame missing.

Little pirate;

you bear no grudge. Like mythical *Jian*,
one-eyed, one-winged; you wait perfect
pairing. Gifts of second light.

GIFT HORSE
The Writer's Cabin, Westport

Night rain swells a nearby stream.
Morning greens this Eden,

happy to exist when I've gone,

another life conjoined.

No serpent here to crush.
Blue sky is wide, earth solid.
At the end of the laneway, traffic
throbs to nearby towns, beyond trees.

A lark sings his heart out.
Close by in a field, Milís chews
wild brambles. A rescue pony,
she came in the night, trailer
sludged through mulched earth.

I give her an apple. I am a seven day
Eve. Wisdom in the clean air breathed.
She sniffs this rosy globe,

breaks it in two perfect halves, crunches
on one while eyeing the other under
heavy velvet lashes. I stroke her pink nose.
She shies then gentles towards my hand.

Her mane's knotted, back bruised,
shadow stains original paleness of her coat.
I nudge her towards me with soft words
how one of her kind, carried
Oisín to the Land of Eternal Youth.

I take her photograph, capture her spirit.
As the shutter clicks she moves her head,
a sudden sway gifts me an image.
Two-headed. Her true self. Mythical.

Omen from the gods. Two lives,
halves of the same fruit, seeded
before we were born.

PIGEONS ON TALBOT STREET

Crowds mill quick around Joyce's statue,
walking stick fit to poke some rowdy's eye.
Pigeons strut concrete sky, despite
such noise, don't miss a trick.

All's not rosy, doesn't click.
A down and out, skin-coloured brick
rests crippled legs, flies he flicks
on Talbot Street.

Silver crutches mark him sick.
Dressed in rags, doesn't own a lick.
His gaze travels to a pigeon high
gift of flight no-one denies
crowns him king over all these hicks
on Talbot Street.

BROTHER

Your image comes in on WhatsApp,
a spinning coin. I wait to glimpse the brother
I grew up with, the one pictured in another
photograph. Of us. Inseparable.

Sitting in a childhood kitchen, a half century ago.
Born scarcely two years apart.

Your hands stroke the sheepdog cropped out
below the borderline, but I know he's there
as is the out-of-focus paint-chipped dresser,
clothes steamed over the Aga
radio tuned to country and western.

WhatsApp shows me instead an old man
dressed in a stiff blue hospital gown,
remote control clasped tight, eyes staring
at a television screen bolted to the wall,
unseen in this picture. Nor is the monitor's
trail of tubes. Your expression maps

a world gone astray, puzzling whatever
it is your mind perceives only weeks
since your brain forgets to use the right side.
Mouth sags, shoulders droop like spring flowers
caught in unexpected weather. Is this really you?
Skin stretching over cheeks so tight it hurts
to see, grey hair sparse, downy.

It's evening here in my time zone yet five hours
earlier in that hospital room. There's no one
beside you, no smiling sister in pigtails,
her bare knees skinned from climbing
after you over walls that now seem
too high to scale.

MATTRESS

No use for foraging crow or mistle thrush,
out to buttress early nests.
Wadding from this stripped-down Leviathan
lines our attic floor.

In the small cave beneath the eaves, scarce big enough
to stand a man in – or a woman, come to that –
we eased clumps of speckled wool between the joists.

Now that's done.

Where we lay together,
our fourth bed in as many decades

put to pasture in the attic.

All that remains is this arrangement
propped against the garden wall,
one steel coil hinging to the next.

Vexatious labyrinth for earth worms
or pigeon holes for empty skies?

A blackbird rustles the leaves,

each movement seeds another.
Our plum tree showers down confetti
over grass laced by a late fall of snow.

Topped by a layer of memory foam
our new mattress
takes us even further from the ground
as if, after all this time, we float on air,
like clematis blooming up
its climbing frame.

MARY GOFF
Inchinnan, 1849

I'm a thread in the story of Mary Goff. My needle stitches
over the map of her letters, as she must have traced
the outline of the shore when the *Inchinnan* pulled away.
She left in cold November, when the ground was hard,
the taste of frost on her lips. She crossed an ocean, waves
forming a rolling pattern she braided into her own small
fabric of a world existing beyond the walls of Ballina
workhouse, County Mayo. She hadn't known the comfort
of filigree shawls or how fine lace felt against her skin.
Instead, she'd suffered the sharp prick of hard labour and
a hollow void caused by hunger. Mary Goff was a link
in the chain of young women and girls who sowed
and then reaped the bounties that a new world and a new
life offered. She left in cold November, arriving in
February when the sun shone, wildflowers bloomed
and the air was alive with birds such as the flame-breasted
robin, cockatoos and starlings. I'm a thread in the story
of Mary Goff. My re-imaginings of her life course through
my fingers into the cloth of her bridal bonnet.

BELL

Summons to strident rooms, high ceilings.
Daylight belled into segments.
Scarce on a winter's day.

Clapper on metal; shovel scrape on iced-
over earth. Graves clawed out in blackened
fields, heavy clods on wood.

Easy to stare into futures folded under trunk lid,
calico or flannel, different sounds on skin
to barter harsh steel for gentle cotton

chime, tinkle of soft bonnet. To sail the seas
on *The Tippoo Saib* to Sydney, bell birds
pealing joy in cathedral tall trees.

OAK

Orphan girls knew wire brush on boards
scraped to bare skin. Arms dyed red to elbow,
carbolic smells. Circles on workhouse floors,
journeys to nowhere. Like crows in winter skies.

They knew the sound of sea on timber,
wind lashed rigging, waves washed over hull,
oak seams holding fast in weathers of the heart.

Duir – sounds like 'dear' or 'dour'. Irish for oak.
Trunks carried over the sea, made by a carpenter
(Tullamore) bore marks of his hammer, saw.
Augers for clasps on the lid, locked away lives
safe from prying eyes, salt pooled in groves.

Beams caulked the decks under which they sat,
as if in the woods around Charleville in Offaly.
They tried not to vomit or to cry, not to think
of the future, remember the past. Oak.

A sacred tree. Truth, courage, wisdom.
Strength, beauty, noble presence. Cut down
in its prime to leave so many hungry gaps,
branches barely touching across forest spaces.

Departure

Winter girls, November in their eyes
wait to board on frozen quays.
Colours of new skies, an ocean cries.

Ships slide from slipways like a lie.
A richer life rests across the sea
for winter girls, November in their eyes.

Overhead, seagulls wheel and fly.
Feathers fall, leaves from sorrow's tree.
Colours of new skies, an ocean cries.

Between prayer book pages, petals dry
scent of meadows tracked by lazy bee
for winter girls, November in their eyes.

In the hold, trunks creak and sigh.
Wood contracts, salt speckles every breeze.
Colours of new skies, an ocean cries.

Horizons seem to lengthen into miles.
Weeks to months forsake an orphan's plea.
Winter girls, November in their eyes.
Colours of new skies, an ocean cries.

GHOST GIRLS
Birr Workhouse

Roof fallen in, windows blank stares. Crows
drawn to such ruin, cleave the trees, squawk
swirl of leaf. Black feathers drop mourning
cards on ground fleshed by the destitute,
names quilled in day books.

Fragile as dandelions are the *Ghost Girls*.
They never left these workhouse walls
or sailed away like swans, new lives
packed in wooden caskets, treasures
once upon a time imagined. Unlike sisters
chosen by betters for their better health;

condemned to stare out on winter yards,
fathers, brothers breaking stones.
Splintered sound chips at strength.
Cobweb spun cradles in long nights.

Ghost Girls see shape of small selves
imprinted in straw cot rows. Tattered
breath churn them to sleep; silence torn
by shrieks across the barren fields.
No Rapunzel princesses here, no long hair
gleamed with health to ladder down.

Ghost Girls are deloused, shorn. Thin bristles
turn them into newborn chicks, all eyes,
thin mouths. No princes left to throw gravel
at shuttered windows, all long gone,
cloaked in clay under scrawny hedges.

Ghost Girls scorn a sky that goes about its business,
net for silver fish, starlight over dark earth.
They wonder at a world that turns a fresh sod,

yields wild buttercups, cow parsley. Necklaces
around slender throats, their world fresh,

not the old hag it's now become.

LILLY PILLY TREE SONG*

Sung to a child, tale of a tree, such a silly
Lilly Pilly sounding name. Perfect to screen

out insects, provide a windbreak against
wild hours. Fast grown tree, as colonies,
its pink fruit ripe on the tongue.

Nonsensical words a mother latched
onto as a babe to her breast.

Words to rock a cradle. Be beguiled by.
Rhyme with other silly words.
Dorrha.
Lorrha.

Not parish names like Uskeane where Winifred Kelly
came from. Four months at sea, arriving into Sydney
the Lilly Pilly bursting into summer,
white as the May Bush, or bog cotton.
Skylarks overhead, mosses full blown colour
notes along the landscape;

deep purple base or light green chimes, harp
soft. Sounds a mother might hear when she'd sing
silly Lilly Pilly tree songs, nursing her babe
under its shade. Happiness flowering in her arms.

* *Winifred Kelly from Uskeane (a parish in the barony of Lower Ormond, County Tipperary) left Birr Workhouse in March 1850 and sailed from Plymouth on The Tippoo Saib to Sydney, Australia, arriving four months later on 29 July 1850.*

LEARNING TO SEW

Cobalt rolls to world's edge. Sister
teaches sister teaches sister to sew.
First tack rows the cloth. Ship shears
ocean's weft, warp.

Thimblefuls of sun slip through caulks,
cotton-white. Stitch to stitch, bolt to bolt
as one word grows another, anchored
in famished history. Rain droplets prickle

surface, pock-marks ocean's un-thimbled skin,
back stitch lines, like back stories,
strengthen. Blood is thicker than water.

News of hiring days urge thin fingers thread
steel eyes, spooled out as sharks devour
what's heaved over the side.
Rotting meat, vomit. Regret. Thunder
booms. Lightning cracks sky seams.

The ship steams on through metres of water.
Month after month sewn together.

Fine work means better hiring in houses
fit for mistresses in elegant clothes.
Farm labour, dawn to dusk, is hand
to mouth, back bent over harrows.

Gulls near the shoreline fade. Albatross
span either side of the prow. Further out
towards Africa, cormorants cut the air,
loop after loop embroidered flight.

Sister teaches sister to sew teaches sister to sew.

DRY LAND

Months at sea. Dry ground
ebb and flow. Blue colour
washed trees, damp earth,
root veins. Pressed bodies
pungent weeds between
pages of days, weeks, months.
It never leaves her, no matter
she sheds old for new.

From Cobh in winter cold
cutting 'the gawks off a stone';

her mother's saying still carried
like her sister's shawl.
Neither having further use
for sayings or shawls.

She's heard it said Australia
is like 'landing on the moon'.

A rush of strange sounding words
tilts her this way and that, words
like 'boomah', a kind of giant
kangaroo or 'cornstalk' –
tall but thin, her shape.

And if she has blarney
on her tongue or 'plamass'

here it's 'promoos'. Words
different but the same,
steady this waltz
between earth and sky.

CRADLE

Her world grows round, a nest
soft with feathers, plump sounds.

New moons full breasted, suckled
by stars. All these months, she imagines

a doorway in her body opening out.
For this she crossed dark waters,
forsook her tribe, married a stranger,
grew a babe swelling into her womb
bonny as a rose.

Stirs of life knock on her door.

But the birthing bed is thorn strewn,
each prick felt in the surgeon's steel

extracted piece by piece, bone by bone
through a heart-shaped pelvic cradle,
legacy of malnourished years.

Afterwards she gathers each petal,
buries them in a heart-shaped box,
love and grief, faithful companions.

POPPY
i.m. orphan girls who left Birr Workhouse in 1848 under Earl Grey's
Emigration Scheme

A gap in the fence, a forced exit. Out in the world
bold colour thieves midsummer gold. Shadows
dissolve in a pool of light. Ravens scatter leaves
over hard ground, numerous as those who came
or went from here. This narrow laneway spools
towards the main road. It could well be the Persian
route; citadel in place of steeple above this midlands
town, bells tolling each long hour. Inside the rails
an altar starched in linen. Not one stain in sight.

Stray wisps of grass cling to daisies. Brief glimpses
freedom seeded by birds. Only a stone's throw
workhouse boundaries. Others made it to boglands
such as Boora, woven into crowberries, sphagnum
mosses. Others settled in a stranger's loam.

The worm turns. This bloom remains meadow
rooted whence it sprung, more exotic
among plainer flowers.

Map maker. Empire builder. Crimson
bloods my dreams; summons Morpheus
to pull back veils; senses stored in dreaming
leaves. Moon songs sung beneath boughs,
tales drenched in poppy scent spun by
merchants ship to shore. Past. Present. Future.

Solstice days soon are done, surely as spring shears
back; stems tied like dark-eyed prisoners of fortune.
Second skin mends a broken history. As it must.
We strain to hold the light. It fades into other
seasons where other stories push through cracks.
Emerging from the dust; wave upon wave of silk.

MEADOW
for those buried on Birr Workhouse grounds

Tall grasses, daisy-flecked. Marigolds;
sturdy corollas for honey bees. Hawthorn
reminder of youthful bloom, month of May
blossoms in Lorrha, Kilmain, Kilcolman,
Kinnitty, Birr. Spiny branched crab apple
hedges gnarled like arthritic fingers
don't belong here with robins,
goldfinch abundance. Redwings

bringing strays parish to parish
as stories travel on the wing.
Like Theseus in the maze, seed-threads
root origins. Cranesbill, magenta
drenched shades forgive shadow.

No blight for poppy sheaves. Fire blaze
cooled by a haze of bluebell ocean;
miles crossed over by those who left.
Feathery love-in-a-mist or lady's mantle.
Cuckoo flowers. Orphan girls
taken from their blood kin to live among
strangers. Morning's glory so swallows

thicken the air, high jinks in high summer
between bilberry, hares-foot. Butterflies,
tipped gold or peacock patterns
over clusters of damsel fly, blue as blue.

Scatter seeds in a wild arc, how mothers
fattened hens and fed livestock before
meal grew scarce and grass tattooed
withered lips. Memorial for those

lingered here, warmed winter-frosted
bones. Blackbirds' songs, yellow notes,
buttercup sipping sunlight.

A wild meadow. Praise for those whose breath
quickened stars in night skies.

WORKHOUSE

Were it habitable, asylum seekers would be housed there,
on the outskirts of town. Away from prying eyes.
But windows are blind, doors boarded over. The roof
long fallen in; *Keep out* and *Trespassers Beware* warnings
signposted outside layers of bramble fences. Wild
blackberries glut the hedgerows, glossed as tumbling curls.

Little record remains of the famine girls who left for Cobh
on an open Bianconi coach, who crossed to Plymouth
before boarding ships for Australia. A journey of six months
over treacherous seas, facing uncertain futures.
Once ashore, they received *direct provision*; shelter,
weekly rations. Tea, sugar, flour. Some meat.
Work. No wages given if employed by a free settler.

Scant history of these young women is documented. Shame
scribed by silence. Swallows migrate from the workhouse
returning to nest each spring, to flit between familiar
joists. Unlike the girls who never made it back.

Asylum seekers are new chapters also to be written.
They come into a town, their myriad fruits unpicked.
Their sweetness spills into sullen earth, as yet
another summer ripens, another year passes.

Berries for Singing Birds

Sheltered by holly's spiny leaf, birdsongs
hatch on promises of autumn's harvest.
Such late bounty fruits abundant red
so thrushes full grown, welcome
as an emigrant's homecoming,
return to glut these crimson pearls.

Pierced through, juice spills into slumbered
earth while in the blackberry's thorny tangle,
warblers feast. Wing to wing. Beak to beak.

Old wives ink tales. Winter scarcities.
As if such abundance, like old sins,
must be punished. Even then, juniper's blue
bleed is a truce of feathered music, sung
in remotest places, heard in bleakest hearts.

ACKNOWLEDGEMENTS

Thanks to Offaly County Council, South Dublin County Council and Poetry Ireland for bursaries and residencies awarded while working on this manuscript; the Tyrone Guthrie Centre and The Writer's Cabin (Westport) for conducive space to work in, and to my family and writer friends for their inspiration over many years.

To the editors of anthologies and journals where some of these poems first appeared: *Orbis* (UK), *The Irish Times*, Pighog Press (UK), *The Jelly Bucket* (USA), *Future Perfect* (Poetry Ireland), *The Stony Thursday Book*, *The Ulster Tatler Literary Miscellany*, *Icarus* (Trinity College, Dublin), *Bray Arts Journal, Washing Windows? Irish Women Write Poetry* (Arlen House*), Reading the Future: New Writing from Ireland* (Arlen House), *Linen* (Lisburn Linen Museum), *I Live in Michael Hartnett* (Limerick Writers' Centre/Limerick County Council), *Abridged*, *Correspondences Anthology*.

'Magi' formed part of *An Altered Land* by visual artist David Fox, an exhibition at the Olivier Cornet Gallery, Denmark Street, Dublin.

Thanks to publisher Alan Hayes; his support for writers over many years is deserving of the highest recognition.

Gratitude to poet Paula Meehan for her words; her generosity of spirit is a shining light always.

Also, Dr Christina Henri, Hon. Artist-in-Residence, Cascades Female Factory, Hobart, Tasmania. Her 'Irish Roses – Bride Ship Lasses' projects continue to honour the lives of the women, some as young as eleven, who were part of various Assisted Immigrant Passage Schemes that brought the much needed 'commodity' of young women to Australia. This collection contains poems which arose from my contact with the Headford Lace Bonnet Making Project, during which I embroidered a bonnet, in Mary Ryan's house, Malahide, to honour Mary Goff, who left Ballina Workhouse for Australia in 1849.

Thanks to Margaret Hogan, historian, Birr, County Offaly whose support is always valued.

Sincere thanks to American artist Sarah Siltala for use of 'The Gift' on the cover of this collection.

Eileen Casey is a poet, fiction writer and journalist, originally from Birr, County Offaly and now living in Tallaght, County Dublin. Her work is widely published. Her collections include *Drinking the Colour Blue,* poetry (New Island), *From Bone to Blossom,* poetry (AltEnts, Rua Red), *Reading Hieroglyphics in Unexpected Places,* a collaborative work with visual artist Emma Barone (Fiery Arrow Press) and *Wall Street* (The Clothesline Community Press); *A Fascination with Fabric* (Arlen House), prose and *Snow Shoes* (Arlen House), short fiction. Her poetry and prose is included in anthologies by Faber & Faber, New Island, Dedalus, the *Nordic Irish Studies Journal,* among others. Winner of a Hennessy Award for emerging fiction, she has received numerous prizes for her poetry, including the Oliver Goldsmith International Award and a Katherine and Patrick Kavanagh fellowship. A mature student she graduated with a BA from DCU (Hons) in Humanities, and with distinction from the M.Phil in Creative Writing at the Oscar Wilde Centre, Trinity College, Dublin. Her small press, Fiery Arrow, recently published *The Lea-Green Down*, a response anthology to the poetry of Patrick Kavanagh with 60 poets, alongside Kavanagh's poetry.